My Life's Tape

from the journey of my life to my end of life wishes

Workbook & Planner

Laura D Pusey
Founder of D.I.P.*ism*
Death in Practice
www.dipism.com

The 'My Life's Tapestry' Workbook & Planner

Published by LD Pusey
Copyright © 2021 LD Pusey

All rights reserved. No part of this publication may be reproduced, stored in a retrieval system, or transmitted by any means, in any form or by any means electronic, mechanical, photocopying, recording or otherwise, nor be otherwise circulated in any form of binding or cover, other than that in which it is published without the prior permission in writing, from the publisher. A similar condition is also imposed on the purchaser, student or any other person using this publication.

Printed in the United Kingdom

ISBN: 979-8-785156654
Paperback Edition

This book is for your loved ones, it is the story of your life. Write it for them and those who come through them, that they may remember you with a love that they can share with others.

Funky Lala △ *Mon Star*

Hi, I'm Laura,

The Life's Tapestry books have come about after years of speaking to people who have experienced the loss of a loved one. People from all backgrounds have shared their stories with me, of not knowing how to handle death when it has occurred and the fact that they were never prepared for it.

I experienced losses that pulled the rug from beneath me. I didn't know what grief was and although I had been raised in a household where death was spoken of regularly ...even fondly, I was very unprepared for the losses of life and the secondary losses I encountered.

I realised that I had to put my experiences to good use, so I became a Funeral Celebrant. This means that I can conduct funerals. I then became an End of Life guide which means that I help people to prepare for their final days. I accompany them and their loved ones through the processes of death. I also became a grief and bereavement coach/mentor and I believe that the best form of preparing and healing is through talking and expressing our emotions.

Death is universal but it is also quite a taboo subject and because we tend to shun conversations about death, many of us seem to feel as though we can not cry or express the feelings that bubble away within. This can lead to more sickness and perhaps earlier death.

So let's have these conversations at home, at work and with friends and let's plan for death so that when we are faced with it, we are truly ready.

Life is for living, let's not waste it by worrying about death.

This is the life story of:

....

(full name)

Contributions to this information have been provided by:

....

The following information was recorded by:

....

....

....

My Life's Tapestry Workbook

Working through this book within a small, closed group of people can be a very invigorating and encouraging experience. We cover the aspects of dying and death that we often rather avoid. Sharing the stories of our lives with others can help us all to remember and even reframe our life experiences.

Many people have gone through the same types of happiness or hardships as we have. We all handle our life events in different ways. How we navigate our joy and our obstacles is what life is all about.

Just look at all of the songs and films that mirror the everyday events that we can personally identify with. Conversations about the times we have had can help us all to come to a greater awareness about the events we have witnessed or endured during our lives. Hearing the experiences of others can also jog our minds as old songs or world events are recalled.

For example: *What were you doing when you learned of the events unfolding in America on the 11th of September 2001? Where did you work? Where did you live? On this day the lives of many people in America and around the world were changed forever. Thinking back, ...did 911 affect you?*

Answers to questions such as these are loaded with information that can tell your future generations where you were at that time.

A quick google search reveals that the Number 1 hit song in the UK when 911 happened was Bob the Builder by Mambo No5. The weather in London was warm and sunny. Looking back on that time might just show you how far you have come since 2001.

How to use this book

This book is divided into ten parts and it is very easy to write in. Whether you use it as a written guide for your loved ones, or to form an agenda for a family meeting, you will find that it will raise many thoughts in your mind that you may never have considered before.

My Life's Tapestry can also be used as a guide for the information you wish to relay to your family in another way. For example, you may want to create a series of videos or voice recordings. You can use this book as a template for your expressions.

With family in mind, this book is designed to be used to facilitate conversations and strengthen loving bonds. Life is so much easier when we have had the important conversations about death. For this reason, it is suggested that you work through the book with your loved ones, a special person, or a friend.

You may want to ask someone to keep the book for you; and to enter details on your behalf, as they ask you questions about your life. That way someone you know and trust can provide the book when it is needed and you won't have to worry about losing it.

There is no need to rush through this book, the idea is to add to it as memories spring to life in your mind. You don't have to remember every single aspect of your life. You will find that as you work your way through the book, the important points will be added and a clear picture of your life will be expressed.

You do not have to follow the order of the book, you may find it necessary or easier to complete the second, ninth or fifth part first. However you approach the book is entirely up to you.

Just get started and go with your own flow.

The last part of the book is to be completed by those providing your care, your friends and your loved ones.

This book is not a Will and it can not be used as such because it is not a legal document. However, the book can be used to speak for you during medical situations. There may be certain procedures that are widely used as common practice by medics that may go against your culture, religion or personal wishes. The medics will always do what they believe is right in line with science and the law. Arguments or queries made on your behalf will always be strengthened by your own words.

Let's take the time right now to think about those subjects that we are normally keen to avoid, like the legal or financial aspects of your life. Later on down the line, we won't have to worry so much because the bulk of the preparations will have already been done.

Life is for living, let's do away with the stress.

**Please purchase copies of this book
from the D.I.P.*ism* website:**

www.dipism.com / shop

https://dipism.com/index.php/shop/

Dealing with grief

There are no rules on how best we can deal with our grief. No one can prepare us for the levels of grief we may experience and whilst we all experience losses at times throughout our lives, we are often little prepared to deal with them.

When faced with a diagnosis that signals the end of our life, we will be naturally drawn toward the loss of our future. For some of us, this is a time when we may think of the life we have lived so far and maybe also the things we did not get around to doing.

Until we actually die, we are alive! Sharing our thoughts and talking about our feelings and concerns about the death transition will help greatly. It is through discussion that we are often able to find that moment of acceptance that comes through having a clear heart and mind.

Talking also helps our loved ones to cope with their grief once we have gone. We all take up so much space in the lives of those we care about (and some of those of whom we don't). For our loved ones, the thought of life without us can be so devastating that it affects the rest of their lives in so many lasting ways.

If you care deeply about someone who is approaching their end of life, use this book to speak with them before they make their transition. For the continued bond of love that will never be broken, complete as much of this book in togetherness so that when that transition of death has been fulfilled, you can look back, and remember fondly the conversations and fun times you shared. Use the final pages to capture the special moments of the transition and finally to read all of the loving messages left by those who also loved them.

Let's do this together

You may wish to be guided through this book in personal one to one sessions. We can arrange for someone to work with you alone to ensure the book is completed to your satisfaction. You can call 0208 895 6485 to request a personal Tapestry Guide in your area.

If you feel you would like for your end of life transition to be facilitated by your friends at D.I.P.*ism*. Do feel free to contact us on 0208 895 6485 or click Contact Us at www.dipism.com.

We work closely with Living Well Dying Well and the End of Life Doulas. They facilitate the death transition by working with individuals and family members in non-medical capacities, to ensure all is in place for a *'good death'*.

None of us know when we might make our death transition but it is always best to have a plan in place because the eventuality is something we will all face. The completion of this book helps those around us to keep informed of our wishes and ensure we receive the care we desire.

Whilst we live, let's not blindly experience this important transition caught up in times of confusion, conflict or worry; and please do remember that where there is opportunity, there is no need to be alone, unless that is your ultimate desire.

Life is for living, let's share the experience.

Contents

Introduction		17
Getting started		18
Part 1	My Family Tree	21
Part 2	My Mortality	51
Part 3	Tradition, Ritual & Culture	63
Part 4	Planning Ahead	73
Part 5	My Celebration of Life	103
Part 6	My End of Life Preferences	113
Part 7	My Closing Days	125
Part 8	Planning for My Funeral	135
Part 9	As Time Goes On	149
Part 10	Journal of Transition	165
Condolences and Messages from Loved ones		196

Introduction

Your life is a beautiful tapestry created from the finest materials, and this book seeks to capture priceless snapshots of it. Primarily, this book is for you. You could call it a review of your lifetime, within which you have accomplished so much.

Life is not an easy road, but every experience you have had has been important for the long journey of your soul. Looking back over the journey of your life can help you to put things from the past into perspective and help you to make important plans for the future.

For your loved ones and your descendants, this book will provide vital information that will help them to gain more insight into the life you have lived. The completion of this book is a beautiful gift and an act of love for your future generations who will learn how amazing they are, and their place within the family they are born into, because you lived.

Acting as a guide for your loved ones, this book will help those who care for you to carry out your wishes if ever you are unable to physically care for yourself, or are unable to verbally instruct them.

When we approach our final days, we don't want to be burdened down with decision making or worries over what might happen to our loved ones once we have passed. We can make all of those decisions right now so that no one has to guess at that time.

Working through this book allows you freedom of mind later down the line, and saves your loved ones from unnecessary stresses that might prevent them from fully supporting or caring for you.

Getting started

Let us go back, way back, back into the time before your birth. Regardless of the relationship between your parents, you came to be; and this book is celebrating your life. What do you know of your parents, grandparents, great grandparents? It would be great if you could go back as far as your memories or knowledge allows.

Were your parents married? If they were, I wonder whether you might know the date of their wedding anniversary. Do you remember their birthdays? There are many methods that we can use to explore your early life. Asking other family members, close family friends and elders is a good idea. We can also check on the internet.

So much information has been recorded on the internet, from births, weddings and deaths, to the weather forecast in the country of your birth on the day you were born. You may want to get some help from younger members of the family who are a whizz on the lap-top. This is a good way to spend quality time with those who came through your bloodline before and after you.

Let's explore as much as we can so that we can get a clear picture of the life you came to live.

There are many opportunities for reflection in this book. Looking back you may find yourself considering the role your grandparents played in your life. Were your aunts or uncles involved in your upbringing? Who were your main teachers or influencers? Did you have any siblings or close cousins? All of these people contribute to the person you are today.

If anyone had a significant effect on your life, let's add them to the book. They matter greatly to the story of your life.

Completing this book might not be easy for you. Just take your time. If you are not comfortable with filling in some parts of this book you can come back to them later, or not at all.

This book is about your life and you can decide what goes into it. You can share what suits you and you can decide who sees this book.

Pages are added for notes as we conclude each part of this book. You can add more information about events or circumstances, newspaper clippings, stories, memories or humour. If you wish you can use these spaces to detail special requirements, instructions, thoughts or hopes as you make your way through the book.

If you feel you could do with some help answering the questions, or processing any part of your life, contact us at www.dipism.com.

After working through this book for friends, loved ones or for yourself, you may feel you can help others to complete their books. There is a particular model of practice that is used by the Tapestry Guide.

Join our network of Tapestry Guides!

Life isn't always easy for us, so care is to be taken when using this book with others. It is advised that guidelines stated by myself: **Author LAURA D PUSEY** are followed with regard to income generation, communication, safeguarding, confidentiality and self care.

The D.I.P.*ism*: *Tapestry Series,* guides the practitioner through the My Life's Tapestry workbook so that they might get the best out of the person charting their life course and expressing their end of life wishes. Contact us at **www.dipism.com** for more information.

Each year upon licence renewal, the practitioner is invited to attend a refresher workshop that keeps them up to date with changes within the industry and the social landscape of dying, death and grief.

Life is for living, let's ride this wave until the wheels fall off!

Part One

My Family Tree

Welcome to My Family Tree

You might like to use the following pages to let us know about you. You may know details like what time you were born, what the weather was like on the day of your birth, or how your parents decided on your name. You may like to list your parents' occupations? Maybe you can share some fond memories of your parents or grandparents? Let us know who your siblings are, and maybe a little about the country you were born in.

My Mothers name is...
....

My Fathers name is...
....

My Mothers parents were...
....

My Fathers parents were...
....

I was raised by...
....

....

....

I was given my name because...
....

....

....

My nickname is...
....

My birthday is on...
....

The country of my birth is...
....

Around the time of my birth...
....

....

....

....

The religion my family followed is...

....

....

....

My Godparents are...

....

....

....

....

The names of my brothers and sisters are...

....

....

....

....

My Aunts and Uncles are...
....

....

....

....

....

My childhood pets were...
....

....

....

My closest cousins and family friends are...
....

....

....

....

....

Names of my childhood friends were...

....

....

....

....

Some of my fondest memories are of...

....

....

....

....

....

....

....

....

....

My Education, Hobbies & Career

Let's go back to your school days. You will find that some of your memories are crystal clear. As is often the case, when you allow time for your memories, you will remember events that you can now look back on with a smile or a laugh, and some memories may still annoy you. This is normal, and despite these life events, you have continued to thrive.

Just look at how much you have achieved.

Often when we think of our first paid work, we are amazed at all we did within that role for so little money. We soon realise though that those early years of employment taught us how to manage and served as the benchmarks for our progression.

Do you remember the name of your first boss? How much was your first wage? Did you keep in contact with people you worked with? Maybe they were family members... Maybe you met your partner at work or socialised with your workmates after work or on weekends. It is amazing how much our lives are influenced by the work we have done and the people we come into contact with through it.

Did you start any businesses? Maybe you never worked for anyone and were able to create your own independent empire. If that is the case; how amazing would it be for your descendants to have the map to your success at their fingertips? What advice would you give them as you look back on the journey of your career and what would you have done differently had you known at the time that which you know now?

The schools I attended were called…

....

....

....

....

My most favourite teachers were…

....

....

....

....

My closest school friends were…

....

....

....

....

My favourite subjects were...

....

....

....

Hmmm, thinking back, did I enjoy school?

....

....

People used to describe me as being...

....

....

In my spare time, I enjoyed...

....

....

....

....

My role models were...
....

....

....

....

My favourite music was...
....

....

....

....

My biggest childhood achievements were...
....

....

....

....

My first jobs were at...

....

....

....

....

My main career has been in...

....

....

....

....

I completed further education in...

....

....

....

....

I started my own business...

....

....

....

Other ways that I generated an income are...

....

....

....

....

....

My advice about work is...

....

....

....

....

....

Living My Life

They say that every life is a story and that is certainly the truth of your life too. Do you remember flying the nest? How old were you when you left home?

Life progresses and we often get our starts with a bump. A lot of fast learning happens in our early independent years and when we look back we may marvel over how little we knew back then. For that, you must certainly congratulate yourself for coming so far.

Did you ever marry? Did you have children? These are important items to add to the book because each one of us springs from a family tree that is to be honoured. Indeed we are all different and at times we will go our own ways. We may find ourselves cut off, it happens. However, the tree remains and regardless of the relationships we have had in the past or present day, our very being helped in the formation of our family tree.

Within this section of the book we will chart our family tree as much as we can, and; make note of the celebrations and fun times we have enjoyed with our loved ones and close friends.

Within part 1 we will also look at any health concerns we have had during our lives so far, and; pass on those secret recipes and nuggets of truth that need to be told.

Do make full use of the notes pages throughout the book at times they provide space for more information than can be comfortably fitted on the few lines provided.

I never married / I got married to / My life partner is...

....

....

....

....

I never had children / My children are / I became a parent to...

....

....

....

....

My nieces and nephews and godchildren are...

....

....

....

....

My family tree looks like this...

I have always had a love for...

My favourite mode of transport has always been...

My first car was...

Significant birthdays & anniversaries are on...

....

....

....

....

My proudest moments have been...

....

....

....

....

I am at my happiest when...

....

....

....

....

My favourite meals are...

....

....

....

....

My favourite drinks are...

....

....

....

My all time favourite songs are...

....

....

....

....

The best places I've ever visited are...
....

....

....

....

My favourite flowers are...
....

....

....

....

I love the colours...
....

....

....

....

I enjoy watching...
....

....

....

I love the smell of...
....

....

....

My favourite time of year is...
....

....

....

On the other hand, as a child, I couldn't stand the taste of...
....

....

....

I tend to stay away from...
....

....

....

My least favourite lesson at school was...
....

....

....

I didn't enjoy going to...
....

....

....

I was often scared of...
....

....

....

Childhood sayings I remember...

....

....

....

....

....

....

....

Gadgets I remember using or playing with are...

....

....

....

....

....

....

....

I received awards and commendations for...

....

....

....

....

....

I am very proud of...

....

....

....

....

....

When I was younger I wanted to be a...

....

....

....

My Health Concerns

My hospital number is...
....

My blood type is...
....

I have experienced allergic reactions to...
....

....

....

I never broke any bones / I broke / injured my...
....

....

....

I have had hospital stays for...
....

....

....

These hereditary illnesses run in the family...

....

....

....

....

I am / was / was not a smoker.

I am / was / was not a drinker.

I did / do / do not enjoy exercise.

I am / am not a healthy eater.

I am / am not in good general health.

I also experienced...

....

....

....

....

Notes

Notes

Notes

49

Part Two

My Mortality

My Mortality

It is very easy to forget that we are alive. Let's take some time now to consider the fact that we are breathing. Take a breath in as far as you can, don't stress over how much air you take in. Just allow your body to breathe and then to release. The breath is our link to life, through it, all else flows and when the breath is no more all else ceases to be.

We can get caught up in living from day to day. Working, parenting and socialising keeps us so busy at times that we seldom stop to consider the direction our lives are going in. Let us take some time now to be consciously aware of the fact that we are alive and let's consider the direction our lives are going in.

You may want to take some time now to consider the following questions.

Am I happy, and loving myself?

Is my life flowing in a direction that brings me comfort?

Do I bring comfort or joy to those around me?

Am I able to feel proud of myself?

Have I used my experiences to better my life?

Do I spend my time effectively?

Do I allow myself the time I need to check in with myself?

Do I enjoy myself?

Am I doing all I can to keep good health?

Am I taking the time to nurture that which matters most to me?

What do I have time to change or amend?

How do I measure the quality of my life?

How can I make the most of the time I have left?

If I were to die tomorrow, could I truly say today... that I lived?

My thoughts of my death are...
....
....
....
....

My thoughts of reincarnation or afterlife are...
....
....
....
....

If I could speak to 4 people who have passed they would be...

My childhood experiences of death...

The hardest loss I dealt with was...

What I needed most at that time was...

I've handled my personal grief by...

My concerns about my dying and death are...

....

....

....

....

What I have learned about life is that...

....

....

....

....

What I have learned about death is that...

....

....

....

....

My thoughts on blood and organ donation are...

....

....

....

....

....

I would / would not like to donate my organs.

Specifically, I would be happy to donate my...

....

....

....

....

....

Notes

Notes

Notes

Part Three

Tradition Ritual & Culture

Tradition, Ritual & Culture

Many of us have been raised with tradition, ritual and culture. A lot of practices that form our daily life are rooted in belief systems that have been created for our survival.

We are taught how to behave from the moment we are born and like sponges we have learned by mimicking those who have been responsible for our care, from our family members to our religious and secular teachers.

Images also play an important role in the education of our socialisation. Through our media, we gain an understanding of what is and is not acceptable behaviour in society and we strive to stay within the boundaries of what we perceive to be good and bad. Of course, our intention is to live for a long time so we don't want to rock the boat.

At times we may carry charms for good luck or recite particular prayers to ward off evil. Many people the world over participate in practices that celebrate birth, life and death. There are times during the year when energies are higher than others due to astrological alignments and we practice age-old rituals that are intended to assure us safe passage in both this life and the next...

Whether you follow a religious or spiritual way or not, you will be able to identify with the activities of others because belief and behaviour is all around us; governing actions and decisions regardless of whether we acknowledge them or not.

Death practices of my culture are...

....

....

....

....

....

....

....

My religious considerations around death are...

....

....

....

....

....

....

....

My spiritual considerations around death are...

....

....

....

....

....

....

....

My Humanist considerations around death are...

....

....

....

....

....

....

....

My thoughts of reincarnation are...

....

....

....

....

....

....

....

My personal thoughts about ritual and tradition are...

....

....

....

....

....

....

....

Notes

Notes

Notes

Part Four

Planning Ahead

Planning Ahead

Within this part of the book we clarify our legal and financial status and set our material end-of-life desires.

Let's take it slow and let's not pretend that this is easy, it seldom is. That is why so few people plan for their death. We can work at your pace and we will take our breaks whenever you like.

Studies show that transitions and funerals that have been planned for, tend to happen more easily, with less stress and confusion. So many people wish that conversations had taken place; and plans had been made in advance. Let's work together to minimise the worry, fear and confusion. If your wishes are written down, then all efforts can be made to ensure you receive the treatment you desire and the celebration of life that you deserve.

This book tells your story. Those who follow you will be able to look back on your life, continue to learn of your greatness and pass your experiences down through the generations. It is in that sense that we never really die, we live in the hearts and minds of those who fondly remember and lovingly speak of us.

So let's get all of that legal stuff out of the way. Have you written your Will? It's a good idea, it saves a lot of time and grief. This book can not be used as a Will because it is not a legal document.

You may not think you have anything of worth to leave to anyone else, but you would be surprised at just how much the government and others are willing to take if you have not officially assigned your physical possessions to the ones you love.

When writing your Will, you will need to assign an Executor and someone to act as your Power of Attorney. It would be a good idea to speak to a solicitor or someone who specialises in Wills, Estate and Probate.

If you have young ones you may need to assign guardians for them. Guardians are not necessarily godparent's or family members. It is really important that you officially appoint people you know who will love, provide for and guide your children as you would. Let's take this time to seriously consider our little ones, their personalities and their needs. Make note of any special care they might need in your absence so that they can be loved and cared for just as you wish.

It might be a good idea to make a note of your banking details and pin numbers. This is information that can be included in your Will. Remember some of this planning is for events that will take place once you have made your transition.

Let's also tackle that other elephant... *MONEY!* Let's speak openly about the arrangements you have made to financially facilitate your care, the funeral services and rites of passage that carry a cost. Death can place such a financial strain on our families that we can alleviate here and now.

We don't have to do this all at once, but let's do it.

Financial Preparations

Talking about our death and the financial arrangements that we have made in advance will not hasten our death. It will not give rise to murderous thoughts from our loved ones and it doesn't have to change the way that we are viewed or cared for toward the end of our lives.

We have all heard it said, that we can't take our money with us. What we can do is make sure it is appropriately apportioned and used to facilitate our wishes for the future.

Openly addressing the matter of money will minimise conflicts and upsets within the family. Some people experience poverty after the death of a loved one because conversations about money didn't happen, and plans were not put in place to ensure all would be well.

Family members will have to adjust to a new life without you and this transition can create new fears, debts and responsibilities. Likewise, there is also a chance of fresh new beginnings and a rise in comfort and social mobility for those you leave behind.

You don't have to write all of your financial details in this book, it may be wise to share them verbally with a trusted person in your life or a person acting within an official capacity. Let's just be honest, any information you can offer is necessary and can change the lives of those you love for the better.

Let's stop wondering how things will be when we are gone.

I have the following life insurance policies with…

....

....

....

....

....

Premium bonds and certificates are located in…

....

....

....

....

Bank and savings account details are…

....

....

....

....

Localised benevolent funds...

....

....

....

....

My funeral plan is held by...

....

....

....

....

Any cash kept at home is located...
    (You don't have to write it down, but do tell someone you trust.)

....

....

....

....

I have / have not put money aside for my funeral.

I have / have not purchased my burial plot.

The address / location of the burial plot is...

....

....

....

....

Preparing your finances allows you the confidence of knowing that those you care for will be provided for. Death does not discriminate, so now is a good time to get your finances in order. It takes very little on a weekly or monthly basis to start a savings pot and it's a positive action when families, friends or colleagues start to save together.

Even if your funeral is fully covered; imagine how nice it would be for your loved ones to be presented with little windfalls because you were able to set aside your change or larger monies for that rainy day.

Having financial resources that can be passed down through your descendants forms the accumulation of generational wealth. With it, each generation can develop and grow; but it has to start from somewhere. Let it start with you...

Writing Your Will

You can write your own Will. It is still good practice though, to ensure all is present and correct with an expert consultant in Wills, Probate and Estate planning.

The following information will provide some clarity on what information is necessary for a basic will:

A Will (Last Will & Testament) is a statement of what should be done with your property after you die.

A Will is an advance decision to consent to or refuse certain types of medical treatment.

A Will allows decisions to be made on your behalf when your circumstances restrict you from giving consent.

A Will can be used to refuse medical treatment or action that you object to on religious grounds.

However, in the event of an appeal made on your behalf for life-extending treatment to be administered; the Court may decide whether to override your wishes and permit treatment.

Note: Your Will does not allow you a legal 'right to die'.

To date in England and Wales, suicide is no longer a punishable offence. However, **assisting another person to die is unlawful.** Taking active steps in any way, to bring about, hasten or initiate the death of another person is illegal.

A Will Allows:

When it comes to the matter of consent or the refusal of general life-sustaining treatment.

If you suffer from a specific illness such as:
- A brain injury
- A neuro-degenerative disease
- Dementia
- Heart disease
- Cancer
- Diabetes
- Disease of the kidney or liver

You can confirm your desire for treatment that may dim your pain and suffering, even if it has the effect of shortening your life.

Your Will can not be used as a legal document to force the hand of a medical expert to administer medication that will hasten your death.

You can not use your Will to specify which treatment you receive, and you can not refuse care that is intended to keep you clean or comfortable.

For more information please do contact an expert in Wills. You will then be able to discuss your options during conversations that will produce a tailor-made Will and testament that gives you greater peace of mind.

Let's bite that bullet and get it done.

Basic Information

My Next of Kin is…

....

....

Their relationship to me…

....

....

Speaking on my behalf is…

....

....

My Will is held by the following solicitors…

....

....

....

....

My Executor is...

....

....

Their relationship to me...

....

....

My Power of Attorney is...

....

....

Their relationship to me...

....

....

I have written my own Will, it can be found at / by / in...

....

....

....

Legal Guardians

It is very important to make sure that you have appointed legal guardians over your children. We can not assume that they will be automatically cared for by our chosen godparents, close friends or family members. Until the age of 18, your child will have to be provided for. This is a legal requirement.

If you are helping someone to complete this book, you may think that you yourself are too young to consider writing your own Will. You are never too young and if you have children and loved ones, think seriously about ensuring their care is secured just in case the inevitable becomes untimely. Your Will allows you peace of mind and a less stressful end-of-life experience because you know your children and those that you care about are in good hands.

The agreed legal guardians appointed over my children are…

....

....

....

....

....

....

Considering Our Children

As parents, we are the ones who know the needs of our children. At times our awareness of their needs is instinctual as they are extensions of ourselves.

It goes without saying that we want the best for our little ones. So it is a good idea to make a note of the little things that any adults responsible for the care of our children should be made aware of.

Is your child taking medication? Do they suffer any allergies? Do they need any aids to help them to sleep at night? Are there any dietary needs that should be noted? There is so much to think about when it comes to our children; and indeed those who will be caring for them, if for any reason we are unable to.

Take some time to consider the personalities of your child(ren). Remembering that we are all different, their personalities must be taken into consideration when thinking about who might be the best guardian over their lives. What are their likes and dislikes? How do they deal with pleasure or pressure? Please take some quiet time to explore the impact the loss of a parent could have on their lives.

This may just be the hardest part of completing this book. Please take your time. If this page is too hard to bear, come back to this section later, allow your feelings their space or discuss your thoughts with someone you can trust. The purpose of this book is not to cause upset or discomfort. Let's just be aware of our children and their future comfort and happiness.

Special Care Needs

My Furry Friends

Whether they are furry, smooth or a little rough around the edges, our pets are also very important and they do need to be seriously considered at this time.

You may need for your little buddies to be rehomed as or when you make your end-of-life transition. Being such a big part of the family, they often instinctively know what is happening even before we do! They also provide a lot of comfort and an endless supply of love.

Of course, you can have your pet's at home with you if you choose to make your transition in the most comfortable surroundings of your home. If you choose to experience your transition in a hospice your buddies may be allowed to visit you. Let's look into this so that we can enjoy our special moments with them.

I have decided that...

....

....

....

....

....

....

My Possessions

Let's now think about your possessions, you know, the little things like the iron, your washing machine and the television. What will happen to these things after you have gone? It is true that some of the strongest families have shattered over something as seemingly insignificant as a carriage clock. Let's minimise the grief of your passing by lovingly allocating your possessions now. You are in full control and if written, your instructions can be more readily followed.

Within your written Will, you will make provisions for your most valued possessions. Have you thought about your car or your jewellery? Remember what you may not value, someone else might, just because it once belonged to you.

It is a good idea to create a checklist of your belongings if you are able. This could be fun. Sometimes we don't know what we actually have and it is always a great surprise when we find items we never knew we had; especially if they are valuable.

Next is a general list of household and social belongings, you may want to put a name next to each item. You may decide that the items can go to charity or you may want them to be discarded in other ways. Make your plans known, that way all of your loved ones will know exactly how you wanted things to be after you have gone.

You may have more items than those listed. Make use of the notes pages provided at the end of the chapter and be sure to clearly identify the items intended for specific people.

Let's go through the house

Front room:

- Television ....
- Telephone ....
- Sofas and chairs ....
- Curtains ....
- Rugs ....
- Books ....
- Artwork ....
- Photo albums ....
- Side tables ....
- Lighting ....
- Audio / Sound ....
- Personal accents ....

Kitchen:

- Pots and pans ....
- Cooking utensils ....
- Plates and bowls ....
- Cutlery sets ....
- Baking equipment ....
- Tables and chairs ....
- Food and drinks ....
- Radio ....
- Television ....

Electrical goods:

- Kettle & Toaster   ....
- Iron & Board   ....
- Microwave   ....
- Cooker & Oven   ....
- Washing Machine/Dryer ....
- Dishwasher   ....

Bedrooms:

- Beds   ....
- Bedding   ....
- Wardrobes   ....
- Drawers   ....
- Night table ....
- Lamp   ....
- Mirror   ....

Bathrooms:

- Mirrors   ....
- Accessories ....

Garden

- Lawnmower   ....
- Gardening tools   ....
- Contents of shed ....
- Outdoor equipment ....

Conservatory

- Sofas ....
- Side tables ....
- Personal effects ....

Garage

- Camping equipment ....
- Bulky items ....
- Hazardous items ....

Cupboards / Attic / Basement

- Contents ....

....

....

Car(s) / Motorbike(s)

....

....

....

Car contents

- Glove compartment ....
- Boot ....

....

Motor Home / Caravan

....

....

....

More personal items...

....

....

....

....

....

....

Upon my transition, my home is to be...

....

....

....

....

....

....

Of My Property Abroad

It is not unusual for any of us to have land(s) or properties that are located in other countries. It is necessary though to make sure that any lands or properties are fully protected in the event of our death.

This may mean that we need to get the contact information of the High Commission if the land is in a Commonwealth country and / or provide the details of lawyers or officials working on our behalf in the countries in which our land is located. Be sure to make a note of the exact address to avoid any confusion.

It is necessary to provide as much information as you can to someone who you can trust to act on your behalf. This is information that would be included in your Will.

I have land / property in the following countries

....

....

....

....

....

....

....

Of my assets abroad, paperwork and instructions are held by...

....

....

....

....

....

....

If I happen to die abroad my instructions are...

....

....

....

....

....

....

....

Social Media & Digital Assets

Now, this might be something new to you, it is very important. Have you considered who will have access to your social media accounts? Your online activity forms your virtual legacy.

You may not want to give access to your private conversations. However, it may be a good idea for someone to have access after your transition for a few reasons. One being that they can access all of your contacts to inform friends and family members of your passing. Your most trusted person can also communicate information to those near and far and receive love and fond memories from those who shared good times with you.

If you like, you can put your login details on a piece of paper and put them into the hands of someone you trust.

If you do not wish to grant access to your accounts, list the people you would like to be informed of any changes to your health. If you can, provide the contact details you have for them, that would make it easier to keep them in the loop.

....

....

....

....

....

Pension Schemes & Shares

You may have been automatically enrolled into pension schemes through previous jobs you have had. There could be money out there with your name on it. That money needs to be assigned. You may even have shares in companies that you may have forgotten about or didn't know you had. Let's just cover the bases, you may be more valuable than you think.

Digital Wallets

You may have money in online accounts such as Amazon or Paypal. You may have collected air miles through your travels. Although it's all in the ether, it equates to money or values that need to be assigned to someone.

Intellectual Property

If you have created something in the past and placed a copyright on it, your creation could become quite valuable after you have passed away. Consider who you might like to inherit your copyrights, royalties, patents, licences, inventions, designs, works of art, poetry, autobiography or music.

There is so much to consider and whilst you may not have money in your hand, you may have a considerable amount of worth in areas that do not automatically stand out to you. Get your creations protected whilst you are alive, alert and able. Never underestimate your worth. There are billions of people on earth and you have gifts and abilities that someone somewhere could really benefit from.

My Mobile / Cell Phone

You may also want to think about who will get your mobile phone.

So much of our information, thoughts and data are stored on our phones. Some people say that such devices are an extension of ourselves.

Your phone may still be under contract and so it is a good idea to list below the name of your service provider.

....

The phone may have to be returned to the service provider. Likewise, you may want for your phone to be restored to factory settings and gifted to someone you care about. You may also decide that you would like for the phone to be destroyed.

These are the little things that we don't often think about. The little things matter, a lot.

Here follows a list of items with credit attached

....

....

....

....

Notes

Notes

Notes

Part Five

Celebrations
Of
Life

My Celebration Of Life

A growing trend is to have a farewell ceremony before a death transition is made. At D.I.P.*ism* we call it a *Celebration of Life*. You may have heard other people refer to it as a *Living Funeral*.

An event like this allows us the time to learn of the effect we have had on the lives of the people around us. We can spend some time with those who contributed to our lives and with whom we shared special events and joyful moments. Surrounded by love we can gain closure on our life events, we can heal rifts, we can come to a place of acceptance in the present, and say farewell to those we love.

Such events are normally held when the time of transition is drawing near, but we still have the ability to welcome our loved ones with full awareness of the situation.

Naturally, this is a sad event, however, at funerals, we often lament over the fact that we didn't tell our loved ones just how important they were to us whilst they were alive.

This book can contribute greatly toward the planning of your Celebration of Life event because your wishes are in one place. This means that your family and friends can make arrangements in line with your desires with ease.

Let's take some time now to consider how your Celebration of Life event might look.

I would especially like to invite...

....

....

....

....

....

The food I would like to be eaten...

....

....

....

I would like to hear music, poems, hymns, prayers, chants, verses or recited prose...

....

....

....

I would like to see photos, slideshows or videos that show the times of my life and those closest to me...

....

....

....

....

I would like memories to be shared by...

....

....

....

....

I would like speeches to be given by...

....

....

....

....

I would / would not like to make a speech.

I will / will not pre-record my speech.

I would / would not like for my Celebration of life event to be recorded.

I would / would not like to give gifts at this time.

I would / would not like to receive poignant gifts at this time.

I would like for my Celebration of life to follow a theme...

....

....

....

....

I would like to see the following colours in decoration or worn:

....

....

....

....

Notes

Notes

Notes

Part Six

My End-of-Life Preferences

My End-Of-Life Preferences

If you are working through this book on your own, it is suggested that you make a conscious effort to take some time out for yourself. Be gentle and give yourself the space you need to really contemplate this coming time in your life. You may wish to meditate, listen to soothing music as you write, or enlist the help of a family member, close friend or official Tapestry Guide to help you to make decisions about your preferred end of life experience.

It is suggested that groups remain small, Although there is no restriction on the amount of people who can work together to complete this book. Emotions can run high and at times like this intimacy is the key.

Planning for our end of life is not easy, as we don't know how or when it might happen. We may feel as though planning for death will jinx us. However, someday we will all die. Visualising any event helps us to prepare for any discomfort or upset we might encounter. It is often said that we imagine things to be far worse than they actually happen to turn out. Our imagination is strong and powerful. When we imagine the worst case scenarios we see them in our mind's eye and attach feelings. Today, let's imagine the best possible experience we could encounter at the end of our lives.

When you have completed this section it is best to do something you enjoy. Go out for a long walk in a beautiful setting or treat yourself to a healthy slice of cake. Why? **Because you are alive!**

Although I completed this book in the year ……………………………………..
Please ask me again. My wishes may have changed.

If My Diagnosis Is Terminal

I do / do not wish to be told that my condition is terminal.

I would / would not like to be made aware of every option available to me including treatment and non treatment.

I would / would not like to receive an estimation of how much time I might have left.

Notifications

I do / do not want my family to be made aware of my diagnosis.

I would / would not like my family to be made aware of my options.

I will make my decisions with my family.

I will make decisions about my care journey alone.

I would / would not like for my diagnosis to be shared with my friends, work colleagues, associates or followers.

My Location

We can not always choose the location of our death transition, however, we can be mindful of the limits we may face within the hospital or hospice setting. At the end of our lives, all anyone can do is ensure we are comfortable. At hospital and hospice facilities we may experience restrictions with visiting times, the numbers of visitors we can receive and an inability to accommodate the company of our furry friends.

If possible I would like for my transition to take place at...

....

....

....

....

....

Regardless of my location, I would like to be accompanied by...

....

....

....

....

My Medication

I would / would not like every effort to be made to extend my life.

I am / am not open to experimentation and exploratory trials and testing.

I would / would not like all forms of medication to be offered.

I would / would not like to explore alternative forms of medication or healing.

I do / not not wish to proceed with allopathic medication.

I am / am not open to spiritual / energy healing.

I wish to manage my care with pain relief only.

Social Considerations

Remembering that I am alive, do ask me how I am.

Please do not assume you know, please ask me what I want.

Always speak to me, not over me, I'm still here!

If able I would / would not like to be taken to gardens for solace.

I would / would not like for my furry friends to surround me.

I would / would not like to receive visitors.

If possible I would / would not welcome conversations on a social, spiritual or emotional level.

Whether I can reply or not I will / would not appreciate words of comfort.

I would / would not like to have periods of alone time.

I would / would not like to receive loving messages.

I would / would not like to be surrounded by flowers, photos.

I would / would not appreciate sounds of everyday family life going on around me.

I would / would not like a television or radio in my room.

I would like to hear……. music / prayers / chants / gospel / hymns / meditation or soothing music / services / books / silence / nature sounds, such as bird song.

I would / would not like for the windows to be open.

I would / would not like my room to be dark / light.

Please do / do not hold my hand.

I may / may not want to be lightly stroked or massaged.

Culture, Tradition & Rites

I would like to have the following cultural traditions followed as much as possible...

....

....

....

....

....

....

....

Donations & Research

I would like to donate the following organs to...

....

....

....

....

....

Notes

Notes

Notes

Part Seven

My Closing Days

My Closing Days

This is an important part of our lives that we often fail to think about. Thoughts of our actual death may be painful to contemplate. However, small details mean a lot at this time and setting out our desires in advance can contribute greatly to our having a calm and peaceful death transition.

Of course none of us know when nor how we might make our transitions. Whilst we may wish to go peacefully in our sleep at a ripe old age we can not guarantee that this will be the case. Some people pass away quickly, others linger for a while. As we are all different we can't say how it will be. We may experience pain, not everyone does. What matters is that we set our intentions as clearly as possible within this book, so that we might have that which is often referred to as a *'good death'*.

A great number of people wish to die at home unfortunately many of those who could are denied the chance because of timing or a lack of foreplanning. Make your desires known so that arrangements can be made in advance of your transition.

Task: (15-20 minutes)
For a moment now, please allow your eyes to relax,
You may wish to close them, it's up to you...
Allow your breath to move in and out of your body...
Feel the cool air as it enters through your nostrils
Allow it to escape through your mouth...
Let your muscles relax and just allow your mind to wonder...
Imagine for a moment that you are in the room...
Where you are going to make your death transition...
Are you in a hospital, a hospice perhaps...

*...Or are you making your transition in a room within your home?
You may not know where you are... and it's okay.
Take a good look around the room...
Being aware of the sensations you feel in your body...
What colour are the walls... Is the room warm or cold?
Can you pick up a scent...? Is there a clock ticking perhaps...?
Is it light, or night...? Are there doors or windows open...?
Are there candles burning...? Is the room noisy or silent...?
Is anyone with you...? Are you comfortable...? What is missing...?
What or who are you glad to have there with you...?
Can you see yourself? Where are you? Are you in a bed or a chair?
Are you aware of what is happening around you...?
Are people talking to you or over you...? How are you feeling...?*

*When you are ready... in your own time...
After taking in a long deep breath...
Open your eyes... Breathe...*

Maybe you were able to imagine your end of life, maybe not. Maybe you were able to build the picture in your mind, maybe not. Maybe your senses picked up scents or sounds. Whether they did or not, what matters is that you had some time to consider your end of life. However your experience was, is okay.

As you complete this book, it is a good idea to think forward as we have just done. This will help to locate the areas in your body and mind that create feelings of discomfort around events that have taken place in the past, or the time leading up to your death, or that of a loved one. You can then address these areas with heartfelt love so that you can find acceptance and peace.

Again, take your time, allow your emotions to flow and be kind to yourself. Every single breath you have is a sure sign that you are alive. So let's continue to live.

Of My Care

I would like for my medication to be light/moderate/deep.

I would / would not like to be as conscious and natural as possible.

I would / would not like to be spoken to encouragingly as I make my transition.

I would / would not like for candles and scents to be used in my room as I make my transition.

I would / would not like to receive complimentary energy healing.

I do / do not wish to be force fed.

I do / do not wish to be given water.

I would / would not like to be resuscitated.

For the time of my passing I would / would not like life support machinery and monitors to be disconnected from my body.

I would / would not like to have the following rituals performed as I make my transition and or soon after my transition.

....

....

....

....

....

After My Transition

I would / would not like my body to be washed by my loved ones.

I would / would not like my body to be prepared with oils and fragrances.

I would / would not like for my body to be wrapped in a shroud.

I would / would not like for a funeral director to be called straight away.

If necessary I would / would not like for my body to be embalmed.

I would / would not like for my passing to be posted on social media.

Notes

Notes

Notes

Part Eight

My Funeral

Planning For My Funeral

At D.I.P.*ism*, we also refer to a Funeral as a *Home Going Ceremony*. Again, we encourage the use of imagination to complete this section of the book. Through the future pacing of such events, we allow ourselves the time to gain clarity over our feelings and acquaint ourselves with the physical finality of our death, our mortality and our funeral.

It is at this time that we can think about aspects of our lives through the lens of retrospection. We can unburden ourselves from the what if's and why's that we still have time to address. Through imagination, wonder or fantasy we are given the chance to say to those closest to us exactly how we feel; more importantly we can assess our own feelings about our one day becoming the deceased.

During this section of the book, we assess our funeral options deciding who will conduct the ceremony and whose services we will employ. Let's think about what is needed when we plan our funerals. Did you know that you can have a funeral without a Funeral Director or a Celebrant? There is no legal obligation to obtain these services.

This is your funeral and you can have it your way, but you must leave instructions on how you want it to be. You can choose your shroud / coffin / casket or urn. You can select music, and specify the colour you wish your mourners to display. You can decide who is invited and you can write or record your own eulogy if you wish. You may even decide that there are certain people you do not want to be present, and; it's okay.

Regarding My Body

Have you wondered whether you would prefer a burial or a cremation? These are the more popular methods used but there are so many more options as well as burial and cremation. You might like to donate your body to a medical school for the advancement of science or have it made into a diamond. You may want to think about becoming a plant or a tree. You'd be surprised at the different ways people are choosing to rest their loved ones. Not only is there an emotional impact on our lives, there is also the matter of our environmental footprint.

You may decide that you do not want your funeral to take place in a formal setting. There may be an area within a more natural setting that you would rather use. You may also wish to have your body rested or distributed before any service occurs. Such thoughts are at times viewed as radical or improper, but many of us have led radical and improper lives that simply can not be celebrated fully in a formal setting, such as a church.

A beautifully pre-planned farewell event has the power to enhance the peaceful and soothing transition for both the person who is making their transition and for their loved ones.

The wake, in your honour, provides closure for your family and all who knew you. How they choose to remember you is not up to you because throughout your life the people you have come into contact with have formed their own ideas of who you are and how you matter to them.

We can only live our own lives and on our demise, our loved ones come together to celebrate our life in their own way.

My Funeral Wishes

We can not know in advance what will happen after we have made our death transition. We can state our desires; however, once we have passed away efforts may be made to ensure our body is presentable if this is deemed necessary.

Let's also be prepared to list alternative service providers so that those arranging the funeral might be able to fully accommodate our aforementioned wishes. Stating our wishes allows for adequate planning and all efforts to be made for a funeral that is in close alignment with what we want.

I would like for my body to be dressed in...

....

....

....

If possible I would / would not like to have make-up used.

If necessary I would / would not like for my body to be embalmed.

I would / would not like for my body to be viewed by extended family and friends whilst at home or at the funeral directors.

I would / would not like for my casket to be opened during my funeral service.

I would / would not like people to place objects in my casket.

I would like my family members to wear a touch of...

....

....

I would like the procession to leave from...

....

....

I would like my funeral to be conducted at...

....

....

....

I would like to use the services of the following funeral directors...

....

....

....

I would like my service to be conducted by...

....

....

....

I would like a traditional hearse / horse and carriage / or...

....

....

....

I will not be using the services of a Funeral Director, I will...

....

....

....

I have decided to have a Direct Cremation...

....

....

....

I would / would not like to have drummers / live singers / choir.

I would / would not like scriptures / prayers / poems recited.

I am not at all religious, I would like a Humanist funeral.

I would / would not like for my casket or urn to be personalised...

....

....

....

....

I would like my body to be laid to rest at the following location:

....

....

....

....

....

The following people are not welcome at my funeral:
....

....

....

....

....

I would / would not like for a loved one to be present at my cremation.

I would like my ashes to be...
....

....

....

....

....

....

Of My Wake

If this book is to be used for family, friends or colleagues to send their condolences at my wake.

Please note: A thick elastic band or ribbon can easily be used to protect the main contents of this book from prying eyes. This book can also be held by an appointed person whilst condolences are being scribed.

I would / would not like to have a video or audio recording of myself speaking to those present at my wake.

....

....

....

I would like the following words to be recited on my behalf...
        (Make use of the notes page and add extra pages if needed)

....

....

....

....

....

Notes

Notes

Notes

Part Nine

As Time Goes on

As Time Goes On...

Whilst it is encouraged that this book be completed when you are in relatively good health, this section of the book is best left until the time when your death transition is drawing near. Whilst you are able to reflect on your life and tie up those loose ends.

Whilst reflecting on your amazing life you can feel truly proud at this point of the book, recognising the grand tapestry you have created throughout this beautiful journey we call life.

Maybe you can sum up your life through themes, cycles or patterns that have been highlighted to you as you complete this book. Let us know the secret to your happiness, your successes and how you dealt with disappointments or hard times. Your words will serve as a great source of inspiration to your loved ones and your future generations forevermore.

I would like for my headstone / tombstone epitaph or plaque to say...

....

....

....

....

....

On the anniversaries of my transition, please...

....

....

....

....

....

....

....

....

Remember me when...

....

....

....

....

....

Thoughts on my life thus far...

What I know to be true...

Desires for my family's future are...

....

....

....

....

....

....

....

My wish for my partner is...

....

....

....

....

....

....

....

Messages for my (Grand) children are...

Things I would have liked to have achieved before now...

The best advice I have been given is...

The best advice I can offer is...

....

....

....

....

....

The recipe of life - The secret ingredient was... hint's tips' & hacks...

....

....

....

....

....

....

....

....

My words of encouragement to the members of my family...

....

....

....

....

....

....

....

Words of encouragement to my friends...

....

....

....

....

....

....

....

Doing Your Bit

Sadly, many strong families fall apart when a loved one passes away.

There are many people whose lives have been negatively affected by the fact that certain truths will never be told. Often there are more questions left than answers; and for those making their transition, there may be an emotionally impacted level of fear that can be eased before the transition, by speaking one's truth.

What we have before us is the opportunity to unburden our hearts and minds, so that we can make smooth and peaceful transitions, without the fear of what might await us on the other side; or worry over past events that can be healed whilst we live. Living with suppressed trauma severely hampers the quality of our life experiences.

Grief from past losses, whether they be of loved ones or possessions, can eat away at us from within; and open the door to lifetimes of illness that allopathic medication can not heal.

Revelations big and small, bring about the opportunities for us all to heal and progress along our life journey with clarity and a strengthened sense of self. How better is the life of a person who truly knows who they are and what their purpose is.

Your life is a beautiful gift, share it with those you love for generations to come.

Acknowledgement Of Fact

It is to be noted that this book is not a legal document and it is understood that there may be times when my wishes may not be carried out to the letter. I appreciate every effort made to ensure that my wishes are fulfilled as much as possible in line with the circumstances surrounding my end of life and the available resources.

Signature:
....

Name:
....

Date:
....

This signing is witnessed by:

Name of witness:

Signature:

Date:

Closing Message

Although you may think that you are too young to think about death or that this is a depressing subject, completing this book is necessary because the reality of life is that you could die at any time.

You may not think you have anything of worth or that your assets will automatically pass on to your loved ones. Peace of mind is something that you can always make time for.

Regularly return to this book and continue to make a note of the milestones, memories and happy events you would like to have remembered by your loved ones. The book is designed to help you to plan for your future, the intention is never to cause discomfort, upset, nor pain for you or your loved ones. Please remember that you are still living, and this book is just a snapshot of the beautiful journey of your life.

Within this lifetime, you have so many opportunities to display the very best of yourself. Let's not worry too much about everyone else. We all have our own life journeys and although people may observe or comment on your actions or decisions; you have come to have your own experiences of life within your own body.

So enjoy your life as much as you possibly can.

Of all the billions of people on earth, there is no one quite like you.

Till we meet…
OneLove
Laura D Pusey

Notes

Notes

Part Ten

Journal of transition

Journal of transition

What follows is a journal to be completed by those who will be caring for you. Every effort can now be made to ensure you get the care you have expressed a desire for through the completion of this book.

As you approach your end of life transition, your loved ones will be kept up to date as long as notes are taken on your behalf. This really helps you and your loved ones. Hospital notes are not designed for the eyes of those who are not trained professionals, and at times it is hard to get a clear explanation of what is really happening when someone we care about is experiencing pain or discomfort.

What can be noted in the following pages are items of interest such as the medication you have been given, visitors you may have received and your general mood, requests or comments you have made through the day. At times funny little ironies come to us through our thoughts. Those little nuggets of wisdom have a knack of finally clicking as we approach our transition.

Although it may sound strange at first, the conclusion of a life journey can be a pleasant experience for all. There are many people all over the world who can say that they have witnessed what is often referred to as a *'good death'.* A good death often occurs when all has been said and done. Calm descends as any fears, worries or anxieties have been cleared. From the moment of our birth, our end-of-life transition is of most importance. We don't know when it might happen and we only get one chance. So let's aim to get it right.

Carers observations   **Date:**

Carer in attendance: ....

Notes:
....

....

....

....

....

....

....

....

....

....

....

....

Signed:

Carers observations   **Date:**

Carer in attendance: ....

Notes:
....

....

....

....

....

....

....

....

....

....

....

Signed:

Carers observations   Date:

Carer in attendance: ....

Notes:

....

....

....

....

....

....

....

....

....

....

....

Signed:

Carers observations   **Date:**

Carer in attendance: ....

Notes:

....

....

....

....

....

....

....

....

....

....

....

Signed:

Carers observations   Date:

Carer in attendance: ....

Notes:

....

....

....

....

....

....

....

....

....

....

....

Signed:

Carers observations   **Date:**

Carer in attendance: ....

Notes:

....

....

....

....

....

....

....

....

....

....

....

Signed:

Carers observations   Date:

Carer in attendance: ....

Notes:

....

....

....

....

....

....

....

....

....

....

....

Signed:

Carers observations   Date:

Carer in attendance: ....

Notes:

....

....

....

....

....

....

....

....

....

....

....

Signed:

Carers observations   Date:

Carer in attendance: ....

Notes:

....

....

....

....

....

....

....

....

....

....

....

Signed:

Carers observations   Date:

Carer in attendance: ....

Notes:

....

....

....

....

....

....

....

....

....

....

....

Signed:

Carers observations

Date:

Carer in attendance: ....

Notes:

....

....

....

....

....

....

....

....

....

....

....

Signed:

Carers observations   Date:

Carer in attendance: ....

Notes:

....

....

....

....

....

....

....

....

....

....

....

Signed:

Carers observations   Date:

Carer in attendance: ....

Notes:

....

....

....

....

....

....

....

....

....

....

....

Signed:

Carers observations **Date:**

Carer in attendance: ....

Notes:

....

....

....

....

....

....

....

....

....

....

....

Signed:

Carers observations   Date:

Carer in attendance: ....

Notes:

....

....

....

....

....

....

....

....

....

....

....

Signed:

Carers observations   Date:

Carer in attendance: ....

Notes:

....

....

....

....

....

....

....

....

....

....

....

Signed:

Carers observations   **Date:**

Carer in attendance: ....

Notes:

....

....

....

....

....

....

....

....

....

....

....

Signed:

Carers observations   Date:

Carer in attendance: ....

Notes:

....

....

....

....

....

....

....

....

....

....

....

Signed:

Carers observations   Date:

Carer in attendance: ....

Notes:

....

....

....

....

....

....

....

....

....

....

Signed:

Carers observations   **Date:**

Carer in attendance: ....

Notes:

....

....

....

....

....

....

....

....

....

....

....

Signed:

Carers observations   Date:

Carer in attendance: ....

Notes:
....

....

....

....

....

....

....

....

....

....

....

Signed:

Moment of transition

Date and time
....

All present during the transition
....

....

....

....

....

Moments of reflection
....

....

....

....

....

....

Moments of reflection

Condolences and messages from loved ones

Condolences and messages from loved ones

Condolences and messages from loved ones

Condolences and messages from loved ones

Printed in Great Britain
by Amazon